In loving memory of
JANICE DYMEK
2015

Gale Free Library
Holden, Massachusetts

EMERGENCY RESPONSE

SEARCH AND RESCUE
IMMINENT DANGER

Emma Carlson Berne

Rourke
Educational Media
rourkeeducationalmedia.com

Scan for Related Titles and Teacher Resources

Before Reading:

Building Academic Vocabulary and Background Knowledge

Before reading a book, it is important to tap into what your child or students already know about the topic. This will help them develop their vocabulary, increase their reading comprehension, and make connections across the curriculum.

1. *Look at the cover of the book. What will this book be about?*
2. *What do you already know about the topic?*
3. *Let's study the Table of Contents. What will you learn about in the book's chapters?*
4. *What would you like to learn about this topic? Do you think you might learn about it from this book? Why or why not?*
5. *Use a reading journal to write about your knowledge of this topic. Record what you already know about the topic and what you hope to learn about the topic.*
6. *Read the book.*
7. *In your reading journal, record what you learned about the topic and your response to the book.*
8. *After reading the book complete the activities below.*

Content Area Vocabulary

Read the list. What do these words mean?

assess
cadaver
civilian
collapsed
elite
emotionally
frostbitten
satellites
terrain
terrorists
traverse
travois

After Reading:

Comprehension and Extension Activity

After reading the book, work on the following questions with your child or students in order to check their level of reading comprehension and content mastery.

1. *Explain how satellites aid in tracking and locating a person who is lost.* (Summarize)
2. *Why would search and rescue units look for lost items to locate a victim?* (Infer)
3. *Name some things you can do if you are ever lost to help search and rescue teams find you.* (Text to self connection)
4. *Are there different categories of search and rescue units? Why?* (Asking Questions)
5. *What kinds of animals are used in search and rescue missions?* (Asking Questions)

Extension Activity

In your backyard or a fenced area, with the supervision of an adult, pretend you are taking a long hike. Think about what would happen if you got lost. Try leaving personal items as clues to aid in your search and rescue mission. These items may include an article of clothing, such as a shoelace, a small piece of your shirt, or other item that can be used by a tracking animal or satellite to find you. Get input from the book and record your own personal search and rescue mission!

TABLE OF CONTENTS

Imagine yourself alone, deep in a mountain forest. You went off the path to look at the view, and now you can't find the rest of your group. You're lost, and night is closing in. You need a search and rescue team, and fast.

Search and rescue units are made up of trained responders. They are experts at finding and helping people that are lost, have been in an accident, or natural or manmade disaster. Search and rescue units help people stranded on mountaintops, in avalanches, in shipwrecks, people who are lost at sea, victims of earthquakes, floods, volcanic eruptions, and terrorist attacks.

Search and rescue units are usually divided into a few different categories: mountain rescue, urban rescue, and sea rescue. Different skills and gear are required for each category. Depending on the situation, units might arrive in pickup trucks, on horseback, in a boat, or in a helicopter.

The Ski Patrol come on skis or snowmobiles. Other units may arrive at the scene on four-wheelers. One thing is for sure, if you are lost or trapped, you will be very glad to see them.

Search and rescue crews must often work in extreme weather conditions, such as snowstorms.

A searcher works near a collapsed building. Search and rescue crews work in urban as well as rural environments.

Search and rescue units are usually part of a larger group. They may be working with a police department, the U.S. Coast Guard, or a private group of volunteers. They might be part of a police department or FEMA (Federal Emergency Management Agency).

They can provide first aid, monitor weather conditions, stabilize collapsing structures, and load injured people onto transportation.

The U.S. Coast Guard patrols rivers, harbors, and the open ocean to assist those in trouble.

Search and rescue teams work with FEMA to help people after a disaster.

Most official search and rescue units were not formed until the 1970s and 1980s. In Alameda County, California, the search and rescue unit originally helped scan the skies for missiles during the Cold War. Gradually, they began searching less for weapons and more for people in distress.

Urban search and rescue units had their official start in the 1980s. Fire departments created specially trained teams to find and extract people stuck in **collapsed** buildings. When a grain elevator in Kansas exploded in 1998 or when a massive earthquake struck Turkey in 1999, these **elite** units quickly and skillfully located survivors.

Survivors are often trapped in collapsed buildings. As searchers work to find survivors, they must work carefully so they don't become trapped, too.

Search and rescue units are often called to mountains. Skiers and climbers can fall or be trapped in avalanches or storms. Time is of the essence when rescuing someone trapped in an avalanche. If they are buried in the snow, they may not have enough air to survive for long.

A lost backpack can help lead searchers to a lost victim's location.

The search and rescue team looks for lost items to pinpoint the person's location. If the person was wearing an emergency beacon, rescuers track the signal. The position is marked and the rescue team digs as quickly as possible to uncover the victim. Rescuers then treat the person for injuries before moving them to safety.

In the mountains, rescuers may have to travel on skis and pull victims to safety by sled.

Search and rescue teams may even locate and track lost people using **satellites**. In 1972, a small plane crashed in Alaska, killing two U.S. congressmen. No trace of them or their plane was ever found, even after a huge search. After this crash, a new law was passed that ordered all aircraft to carry a device that emits a tracking signal.

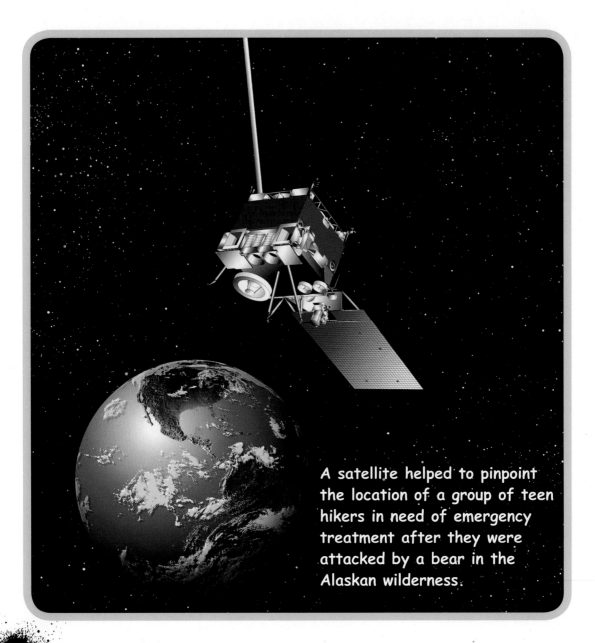

A satellite helped to pinpoint the location of a group of teen hikers in need of emergency treatment after they were attacked by a bear in the Alaskan wilderness.

Satellites help locate the signal, which rescuers use to lead them to the accident site. A quick response to the site of an accident improves the victims' chances of survival.

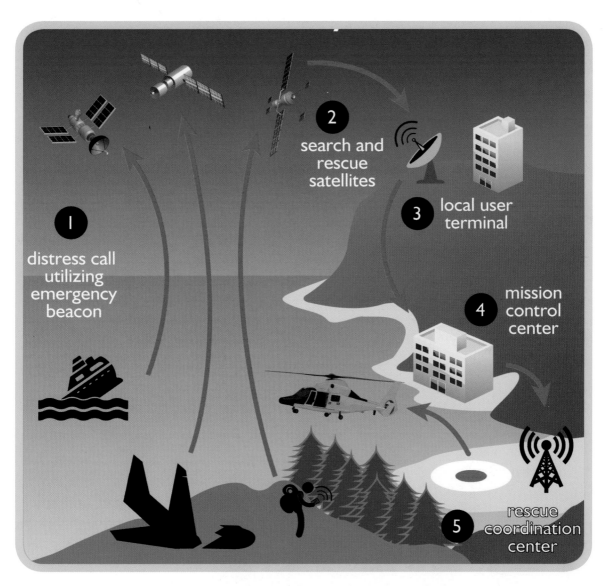

An international satellite-aided search and rescue system known as SARSAT helps first responders locate people in distress by detecting signals from hand-held personal locator beacons or from emergency beacons mounted onboard boats and aircraft.

The gear a search and rescue team brings with them can be very different, depending on the rescue situation. They will bring a life vest to someone on a sinking boat or extra water for someone stranded in the desert. In cold or mountainous situations, rescuers will bring special warming blankets to wrap up **frostbitten** victims.

Rescuers bring trained search and rescue dogs to track a person lost in the wilderness. Electronic listening devices allow rescuers to hear and locate people trapped in rubble. When rescuers know they are going to be at a rescue site for days, they will bring tents, food, and cots for themselves.

Rescue teams need to be self-sufficient and not depend on anyone else for food or shelter.

EMERGENCY FACT

Sometimes, search and rescue units have to search for people who are no longer living. For that mission, they would carry body bags.

A rescue worker holds an underwater camera during a search for a drowning victim.

Helicopters in Search and Rescue

Helicopters are essential in many search and rescue incidents. Because helicopters can fly closer to the ground than airplanes, rescuers can more easily spot victims. They can take off and land from any open spot, unlike airplanes, which need a runway. Teams use helicopters to scan large swathes of ground in the desert. They also pluck people from the sea and mountains, using baskets dangling from a long rope.

Ropes and harnesses to pull out survivors are another important piece of search and rescue gear. Other items may include energy-rich food, water, radios, chainsaws and axes, searchlights, maps, compasses and GPS units, warm clothing for victims, blankets and sleeping bags, portable stretchers, knives, water-purification tablets, and more!

Search and rescue units often arrive at rescue sites in trucks that have been modified to carry their gear.

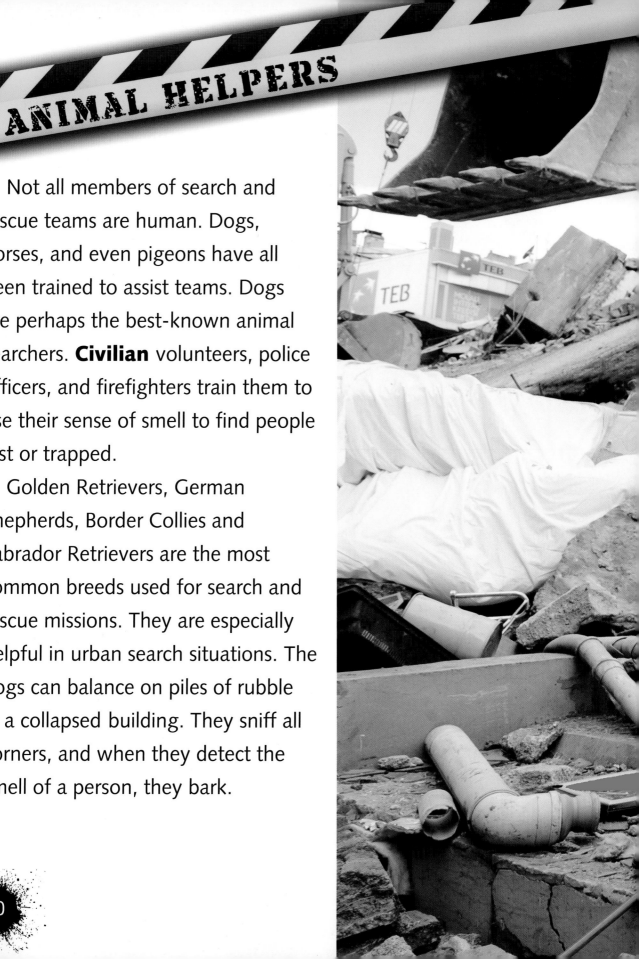

Not all members of search and rescue teams are human. Dogs, horses, and even pigeons have all been trained to assist teams. Dogs are perhaps the best-known animal searchers. **Civilian** volunteers, police officers, and firefighters train them to use their sense of smell to find people lost or trapped.

Golden Retrievers, German Shepherds, Border Collies and Labrador Retrievers are the most common breeds used for search and rescue missions. They are especially helpful in urban search situations. The dogs can balance on piles of rubble in a collapsed building. They sniff all corners, and when they detect the smell of a person, they bark.

Animals can be essential helpers in a search and rescue effort. Here, a golden retriever stands with his handler in the rubble of a collapsed building.

Most urban search and rescue dogs don't wear booties or collars when working. The collars can get caught and the booties can make it harder for them to walk. Some dogs are specially trained to detect people who have died. They are called **cadaver** dogs.

Horses are also useful on search and rescue missions. They can carry a searcher into rocky, hilly **terrain** that is impossible for trucks or four-wheelers to **traverse**. They can carry large equipment that those on foot cannot. Mules are even used to carry wounded people with a dragging stretcher called a **travois**.

A rescue dog is transported out of the debris of the World Trade Center. The twin towers of the center were destroyed in a September 11 terrorist attack.

Even pigeons have been trained as searchers. At one point, trained pigeons rode in Coast Guard helicopters and helped spot floating objects in the ocean.

MAKE SURE YOU HAVE SOMETHING ORANGE, RED OR YELLOW WITH YOU WHEN YOU'RE BOATING, SO I CAN FIND YOU, WHEN YOU NEED HELP.

U.S.COAST GUARD SEARCH AND RESCUE

Pigeons could spot objects that humans could not. They were very good at the task and would alert pilots by pecking a special key.

Becoming a Rescuer

Most search and rescue team members also have another job. They may be firefighters, paramedics, or members of the Coast Guard. Many rescuers are volunteers, with ordinary day jobs, such as teachers, factory workers, and doctors.

But if you want to be on a search and rescue team, you'll need to be trained in first aid and CPR. You'll need to know how to survive in the wilderness and take care of yourself in extreme conditions. Being a helicopter pilot is useful. Above all, you must be brave, resourceful, and tough.

To learn more about search and rescue, visit http://www.nasar.org/

When **terrorists** bombed the Oklahoma City Federal Building in 1995, urban search and rescue teams rushed in to help. They were in the building within five hours of the blast, searching under rubble for victims. They had to rescue people from tight spaces and from high angles. They had to stabilize rickety structures, because the building was on the verge of collapse.

In a major urban search and rescue incident, local first responders, like police and firefighters, come out first to **assess** the scene. FEMA workers are called in to stabilize the structure. Specialists remove giant, heavy objects that block rescue efforts. Only when the site is secure are the rescue teams allowed to go in.

EMERGENCY FACT
Finding injured and dead people can be **emotionally** difficult for rescuers. They sometimes talk to counselors after a particularly upsetting or unsuccessful rescue.

Dozens of rescuers work to stabilize the Oklahoma City Federal Building after it was bombed. Rescuers must make sure a building is safe before they can enter.

In August 2010, rescue workers hiked through a muddy, dense Alaskan forest to rescue survivors of a plane crash in the wilderness. The rescuers found the victims wet, injured, and covered in mud. Then bad weather rolled in and helicopters were unable to reach the group.

The next morning, the fog and rain cleared and helicopters were able to land. They lifted out the victims by helicopter.

The rescuers in incidents like these, are proud emergency responders in the United States: brave, strong, and ready.

This harness supports a rescuer who is assisting a victim into a helicopter.

27

TIMELINE

1915:
The modern Coast Guard is founded and begins performing many search and rescue missions.

1945:
The first hoist rescue by helicopter is performed.

1972:
The National Oceanic and Atmospheric Organization begins its satellite-tracking program.

1940s:
The first search and rescue dogs begin working on the battlefields of World War II.

1968:
John Lawton invents the avalanche beacon.

1983:
Project using pigeons to locate victims at sea is ended.

MAKE SURE YOU HAVE SOMETHING ORANGE, RED OR YELLOW WITH YOU WHEN YOU'RE BOATING, SO I CAN FIND YOU, WHEN YOU NEED HELP.

1989:
The Oklahoma City Federal Building is bombed by terrorists. Rescuers help 850 victims from the rubble and remove 168 bodies.

2008:
The Department of Homeland Security releases the National Response Framework, which outlines the government's response to disasters.

2013:
Researchers at Carnegie-Mellon University test the first search and rescue robots.

2001:
The September 11 terrorist attacks spur massive search and rescue efforts. In the end, only twelve survivors are pulled from the rubble.

2010:
Rescue workers respond to a plane crash in the Alaskan wilderness.

GLOSSARY

assess (uh-SES): to look carefully at something and determine a course of action

cadaver (kuh-DAV-er): a dead human body

civilian (si-VIL-yuhn): a person who is not in the military

collapsed (kuh-LAHPS-ed): to break down or cave in

elite (ih-LEET): very highly trained

emotionally (ih-MOH-shuh-nal-ee): having to do with feelings

frostbitten (FRAWST-bit-n): injured by extreme cold

satellites (SAT-l-lahyts): devices that orbit the Earth and help in a variety of areas

terrain (tuh-REYN): a piece of land, especially natural land

terrorists (TER-er-ists): those who use violence to achieve some purpose

traverse (truh-VURS): to go along or go through

travois (truh-VOI): a piece of fabric attached to two poles and dragged by an animal as a way to transport people or goods

INDEX

SHOW WHAT YOU KNOW

1. What are two different categories of search and rescue?
2. When were the first official search and rescue units formed?
3. What sense do search and rescue dogs mainly use when working?
4. What tasks did the Oklahoma City rescuers have to perform?
5. Name two skills a person needs to become a search and rescue worker.

WEBSITES TO VISIT

http://www.fema.gov/about-urban-search-rescue

www.nasar.org/

http://www.uscg.mil/hq/cg5/cg534/

About the Author

Emma Carlson Berne has written over three dozen books for children and young adults on many different subjects. She lives in Cincinnati with her husband and two little boys. She is thankful that search and rescue workers are trained and ready to respond to any emergency.

Meet The Author!
www.meetREMauthors.com

www.rourkeeducationalmedia.com

PHOTO CREDITS: Cover Photo © Mikadun; page 4-5 © Florin Stana; page 6-7 © CandyBox Images, page 7 © inset photo © ChameleonsEye; page 8-9 © Peter Weber, page 9 photo Michael Rieger/FEMA; page 10-11 © fotostory; page 12-13 © mikolajn, page 13 top © Fabio Lamanna, page 13 bottom © CandyBox Images; page 14 © NOAA SARSAT., page 15 © NOAA; page 16 inset photo © Ciacho5, page 16-17 © Katemcgarry, page 19 inset photo by Staff Sgt. Rory Featherston; page 18-19 © Mikadun, page 20-21 © fotostory, page 22 courtesy of U.S. Navy, page 23 courtesy U.S. Coast Guard; page 25 © fotostory; page 26-27 © Brian Finestone, page 26 © Marsan; page 29 © Larry Bruce

Edited by: Jill Sherman

Designed and Produced by: Nicola Stratford   www.nicolastratford.com

Library of Congress Cataloging-in-Publication Data

Carlson Berne. Emma.
  Search and Rescue: Imminent Danger / Emma Carlson Berne
  p. cm. -- (Emergency Response)
  ISBN 978-1-62717-655-2 (hard cover) (alk. paper)
  ISBN 978-1-62717-777-1 (soft cover)
  ISBN 978-1-62717-896-9 (e-book)
  Library of Congress Control Number: 2014934248

Rourke Educational Media
Printed in the United States of America,
North Mankato, Minnesota

Also Available as:

ROURKE'S e-Books